Dining with the
PROPHETS

OTHER LION HOUSE COOKBOOKS

Lion House Frozen Roll Recipes
Lion House Soups and Stews
Lion House Cookies and Sweets
Lion House Cakes and Cupcakes
Lion House Pies
Lion House Bakery
Lion House Christmas
Lion House Classics
Lion House Weddings

Dining with the PROPHETS

HISTORIC RECIPES FROM THE LION HOUSE

DESERET
BOOK

Salt Lake City, Utah

Much of the material on the prophets printed in this book is drawn from Ann Whiting Allen, "Feasting with the Prophets," *Deseret News*, October 1, 1998. Used by permission of author and *Deseret News*.

Image credits

© Robert Casey: pp. v, x, 4, 8, 11, 12, 19, 20, 27, 31, 34, 36, 38, 39, 42, 45, 46, 47, 49, 50, 53, 57, 58, 65, 67, 71, 72, 74, 75, 76, 88, 89, 91, 94, 95, 97, 98, 103, 111, 112

© Shutterstock: p. vi

© John Luke: pp. viii, 16, 41, 55, 60, 70, 77, 78, 86, 102, 109

© Deseret Book Company: p. ix

© Jos. A.F. Everett: pp. 1, 35, 61. Used courtesy the Lion House

© Intellectual Reserve, Inc.: pp. 2 (unknown artist), 5 (Dan A. Weggeland), 6 (A. Westwood), 9 (Lewis A. Ramsey), 10 (Lewis A. Ramsey), 13 (John W. Clawson), 14 (Lee Green Richards), 17 (Lee Green Richards), 21 (Shauna Clinger), 22 (Knud Edsberg), 25 (Judith Mehr), 26 (Knud Edsberg), 29 (William Whitaker), 30 (Judith Mehr), 37, 43, 44, 48, 51, 52, 56, 114. Prophets' portraits used courtesy Church Museum of History and Art

© Alvin Gittens: p. 18. Used courtesy Pioneer Memorial Theater, University of Utah

© Ken Corbett: p. 33

© Alan Blakely: pp. 59, 63, 66, 69, 73, 81, 82, 85, 101, 104, 107, 110, 113

© Temple Square Hospitality: pp. 90, 93

Food stylist Maxine Bramwell: pp. 63, 66, 69, 70, 73, 77, 78, 81, 82, 85, 86, 89, 98, 101, 102, 104, 107, 109, 110, 113

© 2014 Temple Square Hospitality Corporation

Library of Congress Cataloging-in-Publication Data

Dining with the prophets : historic recipes from the Lion House.
     pages cm
  Includes index.
  ISBN 978-1-60907-917-8 (hardbound : alk. paper)
1. Mormon cooking. 2. The Church of Jesus Christ of Latter-day Saints—Presidents. 3. Lion House (Restaurant)
  TX715.D586626 2014
  641.5'66—dc23
                                                                                    2014012921

Printed in China
Global Interprint, Shenzhen, China

10 9 8 7 6 5 4 3 2 1

CONTENTS

Lion House signature plate.

INTRODUCTION

Whether you're huddled around a trailside campfire, being served by white-gloved waiters at an elegant soirée, or sitting down at the family table after an exhausting day of service and work, the same time-tested recipes—striking a balance of simplicity and delectability—have proven to hit the spot. And no place better understands the tradition of serving up dishes sure to comfort and delight than the Lion House. After all—they've had generations of practice!

The Lion House stands proudly to the east of Temple Square in downtown Salt Lake City. Now one of the city's most familiar and enduring landmarks, this fine pioneer home was originally built as a residence for the very large family of Brigham Young, the great Mormon colonizer, territorial governor, and second President of The Church of Jesus Christ of Latter-day Saints. The house gets its name from a stone statue of a reclining lion above the front entrance, the work of William Ward, a skilled English craftsman.

The hub of activity in Brigham Young's day was the street-level floor, which is now home to the Lion House Pantry. This first floor featured a long and expansive dining room, where as many as seventy family members and guests ate. Other rooms on the floor included large vegetable and fruit cellars; a weaving room, where carpets and cloth were woven; a milk room for storage of milk, cream, butter, and cheese; a laundry room; pantries and cupboards; bathrooms; and a huge kitchen. One corner space served as a schoolroom until a schoolhouse could be completed; then the room was converted into the family's recreation room. Here the children gathered for parties and entertainment. Large steel hooks were attached to the walls for pulling taffy or vinegar candy, and there was a small stove for popping corn.

The second floor included several sitting rooms and an elegantly furnished parlor. Here the family gathered for daily prayer and for counsel from the head of the family. Today the parlor is home to many furnishings and artifacts from Brigham Young's day, including the bell he used to summon his family to prayer. The third floor of the Lion House originally had twenty bedrooms, ten on each side of a long central hall, with a small fireplace and a dormer window in each room.

After Brigham Young's death in 1877, the Lion House remained in the hands of family members for a short time before it was purchased by the Church. Over the next several decades, the building was used for a variety of social, educational, and cultural purposes.

In 1963 the house was closed for extensive remodeling and modernization. After being listed on the National Register of Historic Landmarks in 1964, it was reopened in the fall of 1968 to serve the

The patio on the east side of the Lion House often serves as a site for wedding receptions.

community as a place to reflect on the culture and heritage of the pioneers who had settled the Salt Lake Valley. Today, the Lion House welcomes the public to get a taste of the past as they enjoy made-from-scratch dishes from the Pantry or Bakery, gather with friends and family to celebrate special occasions, or imagine the home filled with the sights and sounds of pioneer life.

In this latest collection of recipes, the chefs at the Lion House step back in time to re-create favorite dishes enjoyed by the Presidents of the Church through the ages. But one of the most common suppers mentioned in the reminiscences of the Brethren does not appear in these pages. Many have preferred a simple supper of a thick, crusty slab of homemade bread—preferably wheat— saturated with fresh, cold milk.

President George Albert Smith was known to graciously decline gourmet entrées in favor of bread and milk. President Spencer W. Kimball even ordered bread and milk while dining at an elegant restaurant in Quito, Ecuador. His wife, Camilla, once told a *Church News* reporter that suppers of bread and milk were as satisfying to them as a feast.

Some prophets have added personal touches to make the dish uniquely their own: President Ezra Taft Benson preferred to garnish his bowl with green onions, while President Harold B. Lee accented his bread and milk with cheese—the sharper the better. President Wilford Woodruff related in his journals that crumbled cheese and green onions were most frequently used, but apple chunks or green grapes sometimes topped the bread for variety.

Of course, Church leaders had to have some favorite foods besides bread and milk. Still, tastes have tended to run on the simple side. Helen Lee Goates, daughter of President Lee, offered an explanation for the popularity of the humble supper: "Few people understood the rigorous schedule the prophets maintained. At the end of a strenuous day of meetings or after arriving home late from a travel schedule, food had to be simple and quick. During conference visits, the wonderful sisters of the Church fed the General Authorities the richest and tastiest recipes. Bread and milk was a quick yet refreshing contrast."

Times change. Recipe ingredients come and go. Health and nutrition concerns differ through the years. One thing that doesn't change is the bread and milk; the traditional Mormon supper still satisfies many an unassuming diner, prophet or not. And many additional recipes have stood the test of time and are as welcome on today's table as they were in the homes of the pioneers.

In these pages, the Lion House invites you to take a culinary journey through the past as your family explores favorite recipes from Utah's pioneer heritage. From Joseph Smith's basic cornmeal johnny cakes and Lorenzo Snow's four-ingredient Yorkshire pudding to Spencer W. Kimball's tart and decadent raspberry cheesecake, your family will learn that across generations, simple, nourishing fare never fails. Add to your own family meal traditions by trying out some of the Lion House Signature Recipes—

classic favorites served regularly at the Lion House that you can savor in your own home, regardless of how far you live from Temple Square. Along the way, see some of the fascinating pioneer artifacts that have been carefully preserved and displayed at the historic Lion House, and learn more about the daily lives of the early Saints and the modern-day prophets—when they weren't eating! As you do, your family will enjoy more than a scrumptious meal. You'll discover a whole new way to come together and turn your hearts to the fathers!

A postcard view of the Lion House.

Favorite Recipes
OF THE PROPHETS

Joseph Smith Jr.

JOSEPH SMITH'S JOHNNY CAKES

In the early days of the Church, finding food was not always easy. Joseph Smith's family had cornmeal johnny cakes so often that one of his children, in asking the blessing on the food, made a special request: "Something better, please, for the next meal."

    3 cups cornmeal
    1 cup flour
    2 teaspoons baking soda
    1 teaspoon salt
    2 tablespoons molasses
    3 cups buttermilk
    2 eggs, well beaten

Preheat oven to 350 degrees F. Grease a 13x9-inch baking pan, or line 18 muffin cups with paper cupcake liners.

Sift together the cornmeal, flour, soda, and salt. Slowly stir in the molasses and buttermilk and mix well. Add the beaten eggs and beat hard for 2 minutes. Pour into prepared pan. Bake 30 minutes for baking pan, 20 minutes for muffin tins.

BRIGHAM YOUNG'S BUTTERMILK DOUGHNUTS

Brigham Young ate amply from garden produce; he especially liked strawberries. He ate only two meals a day, but they were substantial. At breakfast, for example, he often consumed cornmeal mush, hot doughnuts with syrup, codfish gravy, and a roasted squab from the pigeon house. He gave popcorn an original twist by burying it in a bowl of rich milk and eating it like cereal.

1 quart buttermilk
2½ cups sugar
4 eggs
6 tablespoons butter
3 teaspoons nutmeg
1 teaspoon baking soda
1 teaspoon salt
½ teaspoon baking powder
5 to 6 cups flour
Lard or vegetable oil for frying

Combine all ingredients except oil, kneading in enough flour to make a dough that is soft but not too sticky. Roll dough out on a lightly floured board and cut with a doughnut cutter. Place enough oil in a saucepan or fryer to reach a depth of 3 to 4 inches. Heat oil to 375 degrees F. Drop doughnuts carefully into oil, 2 or 3 at a time, turning once to brown on both sides. Place on paper towels to drain. If desired, shake finished doughnuts in a bag with sugar or cinnamon sugar.

Lion House syrup pitcher.

Brigham Young

John Taylor

JOHN TAYLOR'S APPLESAUCE CAKE

President John Taylor, known to have a sweet tooth, was a force in getting the sugar-beet industry established in Utah. This sweet treat was one of his favorites.

3 cups sugar
1 ½ cups shortening
3 teaspoons baking soda
¼ cup cold water
3 cups applesauce
6 cups flour
4 tablespoons cocoa powder
3 teaspoons cinnamon
1 ½ teaspoons nutmeg
1 teaspoon cloves
1 teaspoon salt
2 cups raisins
1 (8-ounce) package small gumdrops
1 cup coarsely chopped nuts (walnuts or pecans)

Preheat oven to 350 degrees F. Grease and flour four 9x5-inch loaf pans.

In a large bowl, beat sugar and shortening until fluffy. In a separate bowl, stir soda into cold water and add to applesauce. Let foam up, then add to creamed mixture. Stir together flour, cocoa, cinnamon, nutmeg, cloves, and salt, and mix into sugar-applesauce mixture. Fold in raisins, gumdrops, and nuts. Divide mixture evenly among prepared loaf pans. Bake 80 to 90 minutes, until toothpick inserted in center comes out clean.

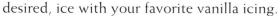

CHERRY NUT CAKE OF
WILFORD WOODRUFF'S DAY

This recipe appeared in an issue of the Woman's Exponent *during President Wilford Woodruff's administration. Cherries have been grown in Utah since pioneer days. The cherry was designated as the official state fruit in 1997.*

2 cups sugar
½ cup butter
3 egg yolks
1 cup milk
3 cups sifted flour
3 teaspoons baking powder
3 egg whites, beaten
1 cup chopped cherries
1 cup blanched and chopped nuts

Preheat oven to 350 degrees F. Grease and flour two 9x5-inch loaf pans.

Cream sugar with butter; add egg yolks and milk and mix until well combined. Stir in flour and baking powder. Beat egg whites until foamy; fold into flour mixture. Add cherries and nuts. Divide evenly among prepared loaf pans. Bake 80 to 90 minutes, or until toothpick inserted in center comes out clean. If desired, ice with your favorite vanilla icing.

Lion figurine, one of many
lion-shaped items at the Lion House.

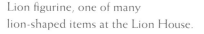

Wilford Woodruff

LORENZO SNOW'S YORKSHIRE PUDDING

Lorenzo Snow, in the deprivation of Winter Quarters, learned extraordinary resourcefulness. He organized groups of men to find work in adjoining communities. The men worked not for monetary wage but for any sort of food staple they could gather. This recipe for Yorkshire Pudding uses some of those basic ingredients.

½ cup flour
Pinch salt
1 egg
1 cup milk
Drippings from roast

Preheat oven to 450 degrees F.

Sift flour and salt. Beat egg lightly with milk. Gradually add to flour, mixing carefully to prevent lumps. Put about 1 teaspoon drippings from roast in each cup of a 6-cup muffin tin. Place muffin tin in hot oven until drippings are sizzling. Remove tin from oven and reduce heat to 350 degrees F. Fill each cup half full of batter. Bake 15 minutes.

Spoons were not part of a normal place setting but were kept on a rack on the table for use if needed.

JOSEPH F. SMITH'S CUSTARD PIE

Anchoring the supper menu at the Beehive House when Joseph F. Smith was prophet was bread and milk with a slice of cheese. The Lion House frequently served this dinner to guests, tourists and dignitaries alike. For special occasions, President Smith was fond of custard pie.

　　1 (9-inch) pastry shell, unbaked
　　2 cups milk
　　4 eggs
　　½ cup sugar
　　Pinch salt
　　Nutmeg

Preheat oven to 375 degrees F.

Put milk in a mixing bowl. Beat eggs and strain through a fine sieve into bowl of milk. Add sugar and salt; sprinkle generously with nutmeg. Stir well and pour into pastry shell. Bake 20 to 25 minutes, until knife inserted in center of pie just barely comes out clean. Do not overcook or custard becomes watery.

Lion House milk pitcher.

Joseph F. Smith

HEBER J. GRANT'S CHRISTMAS FIG PUDDING

Heber J. Grant's widowed mother could afford few luxuries, but even her limited pantry included the makings for molasses candy, a taffy-type confection. President Grant became so accustomed to the flavor of molasses (used in this Christmas dish), he could not enjoy any chocolate dessert.

> 2 pounds white dried figs
> 8 cups soft bread crumbs
> 4 cups brown sugar
> 1 cup white sugar
> 1 pound ground suet
> 3 tablespoons molasses
> 4 tablespoons flour
> 3 teaspoons grated nutmeg
> Juice of 4 lemons
> 8 eggs, separated

Grind figs in a meat grinder. Mix with all other ingredients except eggs. Beat egg yolks and egg whites separately. Stir yolks into pudding mixture, then fold in whites at the last. Thoroughly grease five 1-pound cans (vegetable or large soup cans are a good size) and fill ⅔ full.

Place a rack in the bottom of a large, deep pot. Set the filled cans on the rack. Carefully pour enough water into the bottom of the pot to cover the bottom ⅔ of the cans. Bring to a boil over medium heat. Reduce heat to low; cover pan. Simmer 3 hours, adding water occasionally as needed to maintain level. Lift cans carefully from water; allow to cool 10 minutes before removing puddings from cans.

GEORGE ALBERT SMITH'S OYSTER STEW

President George Albert Smith often ate boiled wheat, preferring whole wheat to cracked. He ate it like cereal with cream and honey. His grandson George recalled waiting through the long supper hour for his grandfather to finish chewing a whole bowl of wheat. Oyster stew was another favorite.

2 cups oyster liquid
1 quart oysters
2 cups whole milk
4 tablespoons butter
Salt and pepper to taste
½ cup diced celery, partially cooked

Strain oyster liquid into a large saucepan; thoroughly wash oysters and add to oyster liquid. Place over medium heat and cook 5 minutes. Add milk; heat thoroughly but do not allow to boil. Add butter, salt, pepper, and celery. Thicken with a little flour and water, if desired.

There are ten dormer windows on each side of the third floor of the Lion House. Originally there was a bedroom for each window.

Geo Albert Smith

David O. McKay

DAVID O. McKAY'S BAKED APPLES

Although he appreciated a simple meal of bread and milk, President David O. McKay also enjoyed the best of home-made cooking. According to Suzanne McKay Adams, the prophet's granddaughter, President McKay's wife, Emma Ray Riggs McKay, was widely known for her homemade pies and cakes.

    6 apples, washed and cored
    ¾ cup brown, white, or maple sugar
    Lemon juice
    Cinnamon
    Butter

Preheat oven to 375 degrees F.

Fill each apple center with 2 tablespoons sugar, sprinkling a little on the outside of the apple. Sprinkle with lemon juice and cinnamon; dot with butter. Place in a deep casserole dish with a lid. (If apples are baked uncovered in an open pan, it is necessary to baste them during cooking.) Add enough water to cover bottom of baking dish. Cover and bake about 35 minutes or until tender. Remove apples from dish and boil remaining syrup from bottom of pan until thick. Pour syrup and thick cream over apples to serve.

Personalized fork
and butter knife.

JOSEPH FIELDING SMITH'S SHERBET

Amelia Smith McConkie, President Joseph Fielding Smith's daughter, remembers him filling the children up with a hearty breakfast. "I think Dad got tired of milk and cereal. Every now and again he would get up early and make breakfast. We would have sausage with cream gravy, then biscuits with our cooked cereal. It was a farm-type breakfast, enough to stoke you up for the whole day."

5 cups sugar
1 teaspoon salt
3 tablespoons cornstarch
2 quarts water
1 quart whipping cream
2 quarts whole milk

Juice of 6 oranges
Juice of 2 lemons
1 (20-ounce) can crushed pineapple, undrained
3 or 4 bananas, mashed

Combine sugar, salt, cornstarch, and water in a large pot. Cook over medium heat until clear, then allow to cool. Add whipping cream and milk. Add orange juice, lemon juice, crushed pineapple, and mashed bananas. Pour into a 6-quart ice-cream freezer and freeze according to freezer directions.

Dessert dish with lion base.

HAROLD B. LEE'S RAISIN CAKE

Cheese was always on the menu in President Harold B. Lee's home. He ate cheese with his ice cream, with his breakfast, with almost everything. His daughter, Helen, recalled, "Mother prepared an elegant white cake smothered with a cream topping and fresh berries. It was a new recipe and she was anxious for his response. After two bites Dad joked, 'It would be just perfect if I had a little piece of cheese to go along with it.'" This recipe was one of his favorite desserts.

2 cups raisins
2 cups water
1 ½ cups sugar
½ cup shortening
3 cups flour
1 teaspoon baking soda
1 teaspoon baking powder
1 teaspoon salt
1 teaspoon cinnamon
½ teaspoon nutmeg
¾ teaspoon cloves
1 teaspoon vanilla
1 cup chopped nuts (optional)

Preheat oven to 350 degrees F. Grease and flour a 13x9-inch pan.

Place raisins, water, sugar, and shortening in a heavy saucepan; bring to a boil and simmer 5 minutes. Pour into a large mixing bowl to cool. Sift together flour, soda, baking powder, salt, cinnamon, nutmeg, and cloves; stir into cooled raisin mixture. Blend in vanilla and nuts. Pour into prepared pan and bake 35 to 40 minutes, or until toothpick inserted in center comes out clean. When cool, frost with your favorite vanilla frosting.

SPENCER W. KIMBALL'S RASPBERRY CHEESECAKE

Young Spencer W. Kimball seldom had store-bought candy or ice cream, but after he married, he and his wife, Camilla, and their children churned freezer after freezer of homemade ice cream. A pot roast with vegetables was President Kimball's favorite dinner, but a toasted cheese sandwich or dependable bread and milk ran a close second. Raspberry Cheesecake was his favorite dessert.

    1 (3-ounce) package lemon gelatin powder
    1 cup hot water
    1 cup evaporated milk, whipped
    1 (8-ounce) package cream cheese, softened
    1 cup sugar
    2 teaspoons lemon juice
    ½ cup butter
    28 graham crackers, crushed
    1 cup whipping cream, whipped and sweetened
    1 to 2 cups fresh or frozen raspberries

Dissolve gelatin in hot water; cool and blend in whipped evaporated milk.

Beat softened cream cheese with sugar. Gently blend gelatin mixture with cream cheese and fold in lemon juice.

Melt butter and blend in with cracker crumbs. Press half of the crumbs into bottom of a 13x9-inch pan. Pour cheesecake mixture on top and sprinkle with remaining crumbs. Chill at least 3 hours to set. Serve with whipped cream and fresh or frozen raspberries.

EZRA TAFT BENSON'S LEMON MERINGUE PIE

President Ezra Taft Benson had a fondness for his wife, Flora's, lemon meringue pie. When he was a member of the Quorum of the Twelve and on assignment in Europe after World War II, he longed for the familiar taste of the pie. He tried to teach the German sisters how to make it. Eventually he received the official recipe from Sister Benson.

1 (9-inch) pastry shell, baked
2 lemons
3 cups sugar
2 to 3 tablespoons cornstarch
5 eggs, separated
4 cups water
3 tablespoons sugar

Zest the lemons and juice them. Combine 3 cups sugar, cornstarch, and lemon zest in a medium saucepan. Stir in egg yolks, then water and lemon juice. Cook over medium heat, stirring constantly, until mixture is thickened. Pour into pastry shell.

Make meringue by beating egg whites until stiff peaks form. Gradually beat in 3 tablespoons sugar. Pile on top of pie, sealing along edges of crust to prevent shrinking. Bake at 450 degrees F. 3 to 5 minutes or until lightly browned.

Lion House plate.

HOWARD W. HUNTER'S PUMPKIN PIE

President Howard W. Hunter's son, Richard, recalls that his father rarely cooked, except for one summer while his mother was traveling. "Every night for a month we had a chopped head of lettuce mixed with a can of peas and a can of tuna fish. If anyone was still hungry, we would break out another head of lettuce, can of peas, and can of tuna fish and make another batch. I'm not sure Betty Crocker would have approved, but it sustained us and stretched Dad's culinary skills." Pumpkin pie was one of President Hunter's favorite desserts.

1 (9-inch) pastry shell, unbaked
½ cup sugar
⅓ cup brown sugar
1½ tablespoons cornstarch
1 teaspoon salt
½ teaspoon cinnamon
½ teaspoon nutmeg
¼ teaspoon ginger
¼ teaspoon allspice
1½ cups canned or cooked and mashed pumpkin
2 eggs
1 cup evaporated milk
1 cup water
Whipped cream, if desired

Preheat oven to 375 degrees F.

In a large bowl, mix together sugar, brown sugar, cornstarch, salt, cinnamon, nutmeg, ginger, and allspice. Add pumpkin and mix until blended. Add eggs and evaporated milk and mix until blended. Add water and mix well. Pour into unbaked pastry shell. Bake 50 to 60 minutes, until knife inserted in center comes out clean. Top with whipped cream, if desired.

Howard W. Hunter

GORDON B. HINCKLEY'S TAPIOCA PUDDING

Although President Gordon B. Hinckley didn't often eat dessert, he liked tapioca pudding. After Sister Hinckley's death, in an effort to be kind, President Hinckley's personal assistant offered to make tapioca pudding. Stir as he might, he wasn't able to keep the pudding from burning. It was a complete disaster, and President Hinckley, in his joking way, never let his assistant forget it!

 1 egg white
 6 tablespoons sugar, divided
 3 tablespoons quick-cooking tapioca
 2 cups milk
 1 egg yolk
 1 teaspoon vanilla

In a small bowl, beat egg white until foamy. Gradually add 3 tablespoons of the sugar and beat until soft peaks form. Set aside.

Whisk tapioca, the remaining 3 tablespoons sugar, milk, and egg yolk in medium saucepan. Let stand 5 minutes to soften tapioca. Then cook over medium heat, stirring constantly, until mixture reaches a full boil. Remove from heat and stir in egg white mixture thoroughly. Stir in vanilla. Serve warm, or chill in refrigerator to serve cold.

Lion-shaped dessert mold.

THOMAS S. MONSON'S SWEDISH MEATBALLS

President Thomas S. Monson is proud of his Swedish heritage. Both he and Sister Monson have roots in Sweden; his great-uncle was among the missionaries who helped to convert his wife's father. Traditional dishes such as Swedish meatballs are a family favorite.

    1 pound ground pork
    2 pounds ground beef
    1 teaspoon pepper
    1 teaspoon salt
    1 ½ cups soft bread crumbs
    ½ cup heavy cream
    3 eggs, beaten

Preheat oven to 450 degrees F. In a large bowl, combine all ingredients and mix until well blended. Shape mixture into 1-inch balls and place in a single layer on shallow baking sheets. Bake 10 to 15 minutes. (Meatballs may be made to this point and refrigerated or frozen until ready to use.)

GRAVY

    2 (10½-ounce) cans beef bouillon
    1 (10½-ounce) can cream of mushroom soup, undiluted
    ¼ cup cold water
    1 tablespoon cornstarch
    ½ cup heavy cream

Combine beef bouillon and cream of mushroom soup in a medium saucepan; cook over medium heat, stirring occasionally, until heated through. In a small bowl, whisk cornstarch into cold water until smooth. Add gradually to soup mixture on stove. Continue cooking, stirring constantly, until mixture thickens and boils. Reduce heat to low and stir in cream. Heat through, and serve with meatballs.

Thomas S. Monson

Pioneer RECIPES

SPLIT PEA AND HAM SOUP

1 pound (2¼ cups) dried green split peas

3 quarts water

2 teaspoons salt

½ teaspoon pepper

2 cups diced ham

1 cup diced celery

1 cup peeled, diced potatoes

1 cup diced onion

Wash split peas. In large saucepan, combine water, salt, and pepper and bring to boil. Add peas gradually so water does not stop boiling. Reduce heat, cover, and cook for about 2 hours. About 30 minutes before serving time, add ham, celery, potatoes, and onion. Cook until tender.

Lion House sterling silver spoons.

OPPOSITE: Photo of the Lion House in 1860. The large west porch under the dormers was removed about 1879.

CREAM OF CORN SOUP

½ pound bacon, diced
¼ cup diced onion
¼ cup flour
4 cups milk
1 teaspoon salt
¼ teaspoon pepper
1 ½ cups whole-kernel corn

Cook bacon in a large, heavy saucepan over medium heat until almost crisp. Add onion and cook until onion is tender but not brown. Blend in flour and then add the milk, salt, and pepper. Cook, stirring constantly, until thick and smooth. Add corn and bring to a low boil. If desired, season with a little more salt and pepper.

Lion House soup tureen.

OPPOSITE: Horsehair chair ca. 1875, part of a set that includes settee, armchair, and side chairs. Currently housed in the 1875 Room.

BEEF PIE

½ cup flour

2 teaspoons salt

¼ teaspoon pepper

1½ pounds round steak

¼ cup drippings (such as bacon fat) or
shortening

3 cups water

1 teaspoon vinegar

½ teaspoon sugar

1 bay leaf

3 carrots, peeled and diced

3 potatoes, peeled and diced

1 large onion, cut into eighths

Combine flour, salt, and pepper and pound into both sides of the steak. Cut meat into bite-sized pieces. Brown in the drippings in a large frying pan. Add water, vinegar, sugar, and bay leaf. Cover and simmer until meat is tender (about 2 hours). Add carrots, potatoes, onion, and more water, if necessary. Cover and cook until vegetables are tender (about 30 minutes). Remove meat and vegetables to a 2-quart casserole dish and thicken the gravy with flour to desired consistency. Pour gravy over the meat and vegetables. Make Cheese Biscuit Topping (recipe below) and arrange on top of the casserole. Bake 20 minutes at 400 degrees F.

CHEESE BISCUIT TOPPING

¼ cup grated cheese

2 cups flour

4 teaspoons baking powder

3 tablespoons lard or shortening

⅔ cup milk

Mix cheese, flour, and baking powder. Cut in the lard or shortening with fork or pastry cutter. Stir in the milk. Turn dough onto a floured board; knead lightly. Roll dough out to fit the top of the casserole dish. Lay dough on top of the stew, crimping the edges to the rim of the dish. Cut slits in the dough to vent. Bake as directed above.

OPPOSITE: Pantry dining room in the
basement of the Lion House.

LIMA BEANS AND SAUSAGE

2 cups dried lima beans
¾ pound pork sausage
1 ¼ cups tomato juice
⅛ teaspoon chili powder
Salt and pepper to taste

Wash lima beans; place in a large, heavy saucepan and add water to cover. Soak beans 2 to 3 hours or overnight. Place pan over medium heat and cook beans (in the same water) until tender. Drain, reserving liquid.

In a frying pan, cook sausage until browned and crumbly. Drain; add sausage to beans along with tomato juice and chili powder. Add salt and pepper to taste. Using the reserved liquid from the cooked beans, thin the mixture to the consistency of chili or soup, as desired.

Lion House pitcher and basin.

Photo of the Lion House and the Beehive House in 1865, showing stone wall and dirt street.

An 1867 photo of the "Big Ten Girls"—so called by their father, Brigham Young—who lived in the Lion House.
Back row, left to right: Zina, Eva, Jeannette, Mary, Maria.
Front row, left to right: Marinda, Caroline, Ella, Emily, Fanny.

HOME-STYLE GRAVY

¼ cup meat drippings (bacon, ham, pork, or beef)
3 tablespoons flour
2 cups milk
Salt and pepper to taste

After cooking meat, remove from pan and measure drippings. Return desired amount of drippings to the pan. Place over medium heat, add flour, and stir until slightly browned. Remove from heat and add milk, stirring well to blend. Return to heat and cook, stirring constantly, until mixture is thick and smooth. Season with salt and pepper to taste. Serve with potatoes, biscuits, corn bread, pancakes, or waffles.

Brigham Young's bell, used
to call the family to dinner.

SWEET AND SOUR CABBAGE SLAW

1 medium head cabbage, chopped
1 large onion, finely chopped
¾ cup sugar
1 ½ teaspoons salt
1 teaspoon celery seed
½ teaspoon dry mustard
1 cup vinegar
½ cup vegetable oil

In a large bowl, alternate layers of cabbage and onion. Set aside.

In a small saucepan, combine sugar, salt, celery seed, mustard, and vinegar and bring to a boil. Remove from heat and stir in oil. Pour hot mixture over cabbage. Cool and cover tightly. Refrigerate 24 hours before serving.

Lion House pickle jar with tongs.

Opposite: Lion House dining chairs were made to fit each person. Some were wider or taller than others.

POTATO SALAD

3 large potatoes

3 hard-boiled eggs

¼ cup minced onion

Salt and pepper to taste

2 eggs

3 tablespoons butter, melted

½ cup hot vinegar

3 tablespoons sugar

1 teaspoon salt

1 teaspoon dry mustard

1 cup heavy cream, whipped

Cook potatoes in their jackets until tender, then cool, peel, and dice. Add chopped hard-boiled eggs, onion, and salt and pepper to taste.

For the dressing, beat eggs; gradually add melted butter and hot vinegar, stirring until well combined. Mix sugar, salt, and dry mustard together and stir into egg mixture. Place dressing in the top of a double boiler and cook over medium heat, stirring frequently, until thick. Chill. Combine with whipped cream and fold into the potato mixture.

Lion House condiment caddy.

Opposite: A view of the Lion House, taken in the 1880s.

POTATO CAKES

6 medium potatoes

1 cup flour

½ cup milk

2 eggs

2 teaspoons salt

Lard or shortening

Wash and peel potatoes. Grate them to a medium consistency. Combine with flour, milk, eggs, and salt. Melt enough lard or shortening in a frying pan to reach a depth of about ½ inch. Drop potato mixture by large spoonfuls into hot lard or shortening and fry until golden brown on both sides.

A cross-stitch sampler from 1841, made by ten-year-old Sarah Matthews, hangs in the Lion House.

In 1907, the surviving members of the Mormon Battalion met at the Lion House.

George Albert Smith at a dinner in the Lion House in 1936.

RICE PUDDING

¾ cup uncooked rice
1 teaspoon salt
4 cups milk
½ cup sugar
½ teaspoon vanilla or almond extract
1 cup heavy cream, whipped
½ cup raisins (optional)

In the top of a double boiler over low heat, cook rice and salt in the milk for about 1½ hours. Add sugar and vanilla or almond extract. Chill. Stir in the whipped cream and add raisins if desired.

An assortment of crystal goblets from the Lion House collection.

FRIED SCONES

2 tablespoons active dry yeast, or 2 yeast cakes

¾ cup warm water

2 tablespoons sugar

2 eggs, slightly beaten

3¼ cups warm buttermilk

6½ to 8 cups whole-wheat flour

6 tablespoons oil or softened shortening

1 tablespoon salt

1 tablespoon baking powder

½ teaspoon baking soda

Dissolve yeast in warm water and add sugar. In a separate large bowl, stir together eggs and buttermilk. Stir in yeast mixture. Add 3 to 4 cups of the flour, oil or shortening, salt, baking powder, and baking soda; mix until well combined. Work in enough of the remaining flour to make a soft dough that does not stick to the sides of the bowl. Set aside and let rise for about 1 hour. Punch dough down; place in bowl, cover, and refrigerate 1 to 4 days. Remove cover and punch down as needed.

Remove dough from refrigerator and let sit on counter 10 minutes. Knead dough slightly and roll out ⅓- to ½-inch thick on a lightly floured board. Cut into 3-inch squares and fry in 1 inch of hot oil until golden brown on both sides.

Serve with butter, honey, or jam.

OPPOSITE: Parlor of the Lion House.

In 1901, the Lion House was used as the site of the LDS College.

FRUIT CANDY

1 pound raisins
½ pound figs
½ pound dates
1 cup pitted prunes
Zest and juice of 1 orange
1 cup coarsely chopped walnuts

Grind together the raisins, figs, dates, prunes, and orange zest. Blend thoroughly with orange juice and nuts. Shape into balls or flat bars; let stand 24 hours. For an extra-special treat, dip the fruit balls into melted chocolate.

Candy dish with lion base
and handle.

HONEY CANDY

2 cups honey
1 cup sugar
1 cup cream

In a heavy saucepan, combine honey, sugar, and cream and cook slowly until mixture reaches hard-ball stage (a small spoonful of mixture will hold its shape when dropped into ice water). Pour onto a buttered pan. When candy is cool enough to handle, butter hands and pull and stretch candy until it is a golden color. Stretch and twist into long ropes and cut into bite-sized pieces.

Lion House high chair.

OPPOSITE: Children's room at the Lion House.

Lion House
SIGNATURE RECIPES

LION HOUSE DINNER ROLLS

2 cups warm water (110 to 115 degrees)

⅔ cup nonfat dry milk

2 tablespoons active dry yeast

¼ cup sugar

2 teaspoons salt

⅓ plus ½ cup butter, margarine, or shortening, divided

1 egg

4½ to 5 cups all-purpose or bread flour, divided

1 tablespoon vegetable oil

Combine water and dry milk powder in large bowl of an electric mixer, stirring until milk dissolves. Add yeast and then sugar, salt, ⅓ cup butter, egg, and 2 cups flour. Mix on low speed until ingredients are wet. Increase mixer speed to medium and mix 2 minutes. Add 2 cups flour; mix on low speed until ingredients are wet and then 2 minutes at medium speed. (Dough will be getting stiff, and remaining flour may need to be mixed in by hand.) Add remaining flour, ½ cup at a time, until dough is soft, not overly sticky, and not stiff. (It is not necessary to use the entire amount of flour.)

Remove dough off sides of bowl and pour oil all around sides of bowl. Turn dough over in bowl so it is covered with oil. Cover with plastic wrap and allow to rise in a warm place until doubled in size, about 1½ hours. Lightly sprinkle cutting board or counter with flour and place dough on floured surface. Roll out and shape as desired. Place on greased or parchment-lined baking pans. Cover lightly with plastic wrap. Let rise in a warm place until rolls are doubled in size, about 1 to 1½ hours.

Bake 15 to 20 minutes at 375 degrees F., or until golden brown. Melt ½ cup butter and brush rolls with melted butter while hot.

Chef's Tip: To freeze shaped rolls for later use, simply double the amount of yeast used when making dough. After the first rise, shape rolls but do not allow to rise again. Place rolls on a baking sheet and immediately place in freezer. When dough is frozen solid, remove rolls from pan and place in a plastic bag, squeeze excess air out of bag, and seal. Rolls may be frozen for up to 3 weeks.

When ready to use, place frozen rolls on greased or parchment-lined baking sheet, all facing the same direction. Cover lightly with plastic wrap and let thaw and rise until doubled in size, 4 to 5 hours. Bake as directed.

ORANGE ROLLS

Prepare one recipe of Lion House Dinner Roll dough. Roll dough into a rectangle about ¼-inch thick. Brush dough with Orange Butter (below) and sprinkle ¼ cup sugar on top. With pizza cutter, cut 3½-inch strips on long side of rectangle. Starting at short side of rectangle, cut 2-inch strips of dough. Roll up strips, starting with narrow edge. Place on lightly greased baking sheet with cut edge flat on baking sheet. Allow to rise until double in size. Bake at 375 degrees F. 12 to 15 minutes, until light golden brown. Remove from oven and brush with melted butter. Allow to cool about 10 to 15 minutes; drizzle with Icing.

ORANGE BUTTER

> ½ cup butter, melted
> Zest of 2 oranges

Stir together melted butter and orange zest.

ICING

> 1½ cups powdered sugar
> 2 tablespoons orange juice, squeezed from zested oranges above
> 2 to 4 tablespoons heavy cream, or 2 tablespoons half-and-half

Place powdered sugar and orange juice in bowl; add half the amount of heavy cream. With spoon or mixer, mix until smooth. If icing is too thick, add more cream a little at a time. The hotter the rolls are when frosted, the thicker the frosting needs to be. For extra orange flavor, add 1 to 2 teaspoons of orange zest, if desired.

CALICO BEEF AND BEAN BAKE

½ to 1 pound ground beef

¾ pound bacon, cut in pieces

1 cup chopped onion

2 (20-ounce) cans pork and beans

1 (16-ounce) can dark red kidney beans, drained

1 (16-ounce) can butter beans

1 cup ketchup

¼ cup packed brown sugar

3 tablespoons white vinegar

1 teaspoon salt

Black pepper to taste

Brown ground beef, bacon, and onion in a 12-inch skillet; drain off fat. Pour meat mixture into a baking dish or slow-cooker pot. Stir in remaining ingredients. Cook in baking dish at 325 degrees F. for 1½ hours, or in an electric slow cooker on low for 4 to 6 hours.

Antique dog figurines.

SARAH'S SALAD

1 head iceberg lettuce

3 strips bacon

½ (10-ounce) package frozen peas

¼ teaspoon sugar

½ teaspoon salt

¼ teaspoon white pepper

½ cup Swiss cheese (2½ ounces), cut in strips

⅔ cup chopped green onions

¼ cup mayonnaise

¼ cup salad dressing (such as Miracle Whip)

Wash and drain lettuce; dry thoroughly. Dice bacon and sauté until crisp; drain on paper towels. Run hot water over frozen peas and drain. Into salad bowl, tear lettuce into bite-sized pieces. Sprinkle with sugar, salt, and pepper. Add peas, Swiss cheese, green onion, mayonnaise, and salad dressing. Chill. When ready to serve, toss salad and garnish with bacon.

Note: Ingredients may be layered, if desired, with mayonnaise spread on top as last layer. Cover tightly and refrigerate overnight.

Silver cream pitcher.

ROASTED ROOT VEGETABLES

1 large onion

2 large carrots

1 large potato

2 large parsnips

2 large turnips

3 tablespoons canola oil

1 teaspoon cracked black pepper

1 teaspoon kosher salt

1 red bell pepper

1 green bell pepper

1 tablespoon chopped fresh parsley

Preheat oven to 375 degrees F. Thoroughly clean all vegetables. Peel onion and carrots. Slice or chop all vegetables into bite-sized pieces, keeping each separate. Combine hard root vegetables (carrots, potatoes, parsnips, and turnips) in a large mixing bowl. Add 2 tablespoons oil and ½ teaspoon pepper and ½ teaspoon salt. Toss well until vegetables are evenly coated. Spread vegetables out evenly in one layer in a large baking pan and place in oven. Toss remaining vegetables in remaining oil, pepper, and salt. When vegetables in oven are slightly tender (about 30 to 35 minutes), remove from oven and add remaining vegetables to pan. Return to oven and continue roasting until all vegetables are tender and begin to brown (about 20 minutes). Serve hot, garnished with chopped fresh parsley.

Any combination of vegetables will work well. Use whatever you like. Other vegetables recommended are zucchini, yellow squash, any hard winter squash, or beets. Beets will tend to color the other vegetables, so keep them separate until served. Remember to add softer vegetables later to avoid overcooking.

COLD CHICKEN SALAD CROISSANTS

2 tablespoons salt

4 pounds boneless, skinless chicken breasts, thawed

½ cup diced onion

½ cup diced celery

¾ cup chopped walnuts

1 ½ cups mayonnaise

Salt and white pepper to taste

20 croissants

Fill a large stockpot half full of water and stir in 2 tablespoons salt. Bring to a boil. Place the chicken breasts in the boiling water and cook until the juices run clear or the meat registers 165 degrees F. on a thermometer.

Remove chicken and place in a large glass baking dish, spreading the chicken out to help it cool. Place the chicken breasts in the refrigerator for 4 hours or until the chicken is completely cooled.

In a large bowl, combine onion, celery, walnuts, mayonnaise, and salt and pepper. Mix with a large spoon. Cut the cooled chicken into strips and mix with other ingredients in bowl. Season with additional salt and white pepper to taste. Store in refrigerator. When ready to serve, split croissants and spoon chicken salad into them.

Note: Chicken salad can be made up to one day in advance. Holding the salad any longer may bring out an unpleasant aftertaste of onion.

LION HOUSE TOMATO BISQUE

12 to 15 Roma tomatoes (reserve 1 roasted tomato for garnish)

4 (10¾-ounce) cans condensed tomato soup

2 cups chicken stock

1 cup beef stock

1 (2½-ounce) bunch fresh basil, or 2 tablespoons dried basil

1 cup sugar (or more or less, to taste)

2 to 3 cups cream

Salt and pepper to taste

1 cup sour cream

2 tablespoons milk

Place tomatoes on baking sheet and roast in oven at 350 degrees F. until tops blacken. Combine tomato soup, chicken stock, and beef stock in a large soup pot. Fill blender no more than ⅓ full with roasted tomatoes and basil; purée until smooth. (Vent lid of blender so steam doesn't build up.) Repeat until all tomatoes are puréed. Add purée to pot and simmer. Add sugar until mixture is slightly sweet. (Don't skimp on the sugar—it may take more or less, depending on the tomatoes.) Add cream to desired consistency. Season to taste with salt and pepper.

For garnish, stir sour cream and milk together until well blended. Place in a small zip-top bag and seal. Cut a small piece off one corner of the bag and squeeze 8 to 12 small drops of cream onto individual servings of soup. Swirl with toothpick if desired. Chop reserved tomato into fine pieces and place a few pieces in the center of each bowl.

Chef's Tip: The soup should not taste like marinara sauce but should have a slightly sweet, creamy flavor.

CALIFORNIA CHOWDER

½ cup butter

1 cup flour

1 tablespoon chicken soup base

2 cups heavy cream

4 cups milk

4 cups water

2 cups peeled, diced carrots

4 cups peeled, diced potatoes

2 cups diced celery

1 teaspoon granulated garlic, or 2 cloves fresh minced garlic

1 tablespoon salt

1 tablespoon Worcestershire sauce

1 cup finely chopped onion

1 tablespoon vegetable oil

2 cups fresh broccoli

2 cups fresh cauliflower

Fresh parsley or thyme (for garnish)

Melt butter in a large soup pot. Add flour and mix well. Add chicken soup base, cream, milk, and water. Bring to a low boil and then add carrots, potatoes, celery, garlic, salt, and Worcestershire sauce. Cook 45 minutes. In a separate saucepan, sauté onion in oil for 3 minutes and add to soup with broccoli and cauliflower. Cook another 15 minutes or until vegetables are tender.

Garnish with fresh parsley or thyme.

Chef's Tip: Two (12-ounce) bags frozen California-blend vegetables, thawed and slightly chopped, may be substituted for carrots, cauliflower, and broccoli.

CHICKEN DUMPLING SOUP

1 large onion, diced

2 carrots, diced

1 ½ ribs celery, diced

Meat from 1 roasted chicken, cooked
and shredded

4 to 6 cups chicken broth

1 cup fresh cut green beans

1 cup pearl barley (optional)

1 teaspoon celery salt

1 tablespoon fresh chopped parsley

1 bay leaf

1 teaspoon dried thyme

Salt and pepper to taste

1 recipe Dumpling Dough (below)

Lightly sauté the onion, carrots, and celery in a small amount of oil in a large soup pot. Add shredded chicken, broth, green beans, pearl barley, celery salt, parsley, bay leaf, and thyme; simmer until the barley is tender. Season to taste with salt and pepper. Add spoon-sized balls of Dumpling Dough and simmer until dumplings rise. Makes enough for the whole family and friends if they stop by.

DUMPLING DOUGH

1 cup milk

½ cup butter

½ teaspoon salt

½ teaspoon ground nutmeg

1 cup flour

3 eggs

Bring milk and butter to a boil in a medium saucepan; add salt and nutmeg. Remove from heat and immediately add flour, stirring until dough leaves the sides of the pan. Incorporate the eggs, one at a time, forming a sticky dough.

HEARTY CHILI

1 to 2 pounds beef, diced (use your favorite leftover roast)

2 large onions, chopped

½ teaspoon cayenne pepper

1 to 2 tablespoons chili powder

1 tablespoon cumin

Salt and pepper to taste

1 large green bell pepper, chopped

1 large red bell pepper, chopped

1 (12-ounce) bottle chili sauce

4 cups diced tomatoes

1 cup packed brown sugar

2 (15-ounce) cans red kidney beans, drained and rinsed

Brown beef and onions in a large, heavy soup pot with cayenne pepper, chili powder, cumin, salt, and pepper. Add bell peppers and cook slightly. Add chili sauce, tomatoes, and brown sugar. Simmer 30 minutes on low and then add beans and bring to a low simmer again. Adjust seasonings to taste.

To Prepare in Slow Cooker: Brown beef and oni remaining ingredients in slow cooker. Cool 3½ to 4 hours, stirring once or twice.

Silver serving spoon.

LION HOUSE RED-RUB SALMON

2 cups paprika
2 cups brown sugar
½ cup kosher salt
½ cup thyme
1 cup lemon pepper

Mix all ingredients together and store in an airtight container. Use as needed.

When preparing salmon fillets, coat each side of the fish with the red-rub mixture and bake or grill.

Wood and marble hutch.

SUN-DRIED TOMATO CHICKEN

8 boneless, skinless chicken breast halves
1 cup bread crumbs
2 cups fresh spinach leaves
1 cup sun-dried tomatoes
8 slices Provolone cheese

Coat chicken with bread crumbs. Spray baking sheet with cooking spray and place chicken on sheet. Bake at 350 degrees F. to an internal temperature of 160 degrees F. (30 to 45 minutes). Remove from oven and place 3 or 4 spinach leaves, a spoonful of sun-dried tomatoes, and a slice of cheese on each chicken breast. Return to the oven until the cheese melts. Top with Sun-Dried Tomato Sauce (below).

SUN-DRIED TOMATO SAUCE

4 tablespoons butter
½ cup flour
½ cup chopped onion
2 cups heavy cream
2 cups water
2 cups milk
1 tablespoon chicken soup base
½ cup sun-dried tomatoes

In a large saucepan, melt butter over medium heat and add flour and onions, stirring constantly. Slowly stir in liquids. Add chicken soup base and tomatoes. Blend with an immersion blender until well mixed. Heat until thickened. Serve over baked chicken breasts.

SANTA FE CHICKEN

1 pound cream cheese

1 cup green chilies

8 to 12 chicken breasts (7 ounces each), boneless,
   skinless, pounded flat or butterflied

3 cups cornflake crumbs

Mix cream cheese and chiles until soft. Bread one side of each breast with crumbs. Holding chicken breaded side down in your hand, place one heaping tablespoon cream cheese mixture on chicken and wrap chicken around mixture. Bake at 350 degrees F. until chicken is done, about 20 to 25 minutes.

Hinged, silver hot-water dispenser.

LION HOUSE MEAT LOAF

2 pounds lean ground beef
1 teaspoon salt
3 eggs, beaten slightly
¾ cup dry bread crumbs
Meat Loaf Sauce (below)

Mix ground beef, salt, eggs, bread crumbs, and half the sauce until well blended. Mold into one large or two small loaf pans. Bake at 350 degrees F. 1½ hours for large loaf, about 1 hour for smaller ones. Remove from oven and allow to stand about 10 minutes for easier slicing. Serve with remaining sauce.

MEAT LOAF SAUCE

½ cup chopped onion
2 tablespoons shortening
1 (10½-ounce) can condensed tomato soup
1 teaspoon Worcestershire sauce
Few grains pepper
¼ cup water

Sauté onion in shortening until tender. Add soup, Worcestershire sauce, pepper, and water. Simmer a few minutes to blend flavors.

BAKED CHICKEN CORDON BLEU

4 whole chicken breasts, halved
8 thin slices cooked ham
4 slices Swiss cheese, cut into strips about 1½ inches long and ½-inch wide
Salt
Pepper
Thyme or rosemary
¼ cup melted butter or margarine
½ cup cornflake crumbs
Cordon Bleu Sauce (below)

Skin and bone chicken breast halves. Place each half between sheets of plastic wrap, skinned side down, and pound with meat mallet to about ⅛-inch thickness.

On each ham slice place a strip of cheese; sprinkle lightly with seasonings. Roll ham and cheese jelly-roll style, then roll each chicken breast with ham and cheese inside. Tuck in ends and seal well. (Tie rolls if necessary, or fasten edges with toothpicks.) Dip each roll in melted butter, then roll in cornflake crumbs, turning to thoroughly coat each roll. Place rolls in 13x9-inch baking dish. Bake uncovered at 400 degrees F. about 40 minutes, or until chicken is golden brown. Serve with Cordon Bleu Sauce, if desired.

CORDON BLEU SAUCE

1 (10½-ounce) can cream of chicken soup
½ cup sour cream
Juice of 1 lemon (about ⅓ cup)

Blend ingredients and heat. Serve over chicken rolls, if desired.

OLD-FASHIONED SUGAR COOKIES

1 ½ cups sugar

⅔ cup butter or shortening (butter makes a better-tasting cookie)

2 eggs, beaten

2 tablespoons milk

1 teaspoon vanilla

3 ¼ cups flour

2 ½ teaspoons baking powder

½ teaspoon salt

Decorative toppings (below)

Cream sugar and butter or shortening; add eggs, milk, and vanilla. Sift dry ingredients together and beat into creamed mixture, combining thoroughly. With hands, shape dough into a ball. Wrap and refrigerate 2 to 3 hours or overnight until dough is easy to handle.

Grease cookie sheets lightly. On lightly floured board, roll half or a third of the dough at a time, keeping remaining dough refrigerated. For crisp cookies, roll dough paper-thin. For softer cookies, roll ⅛-inch to ¼-inch thick. Cut into desired shapes with floured cookie cutter. Reroll trimmings and cut.

Place cookies half an inch apart on cookie sheets. Sprinkle with decorative toppings, if desired. Bake at 375 degrees F. about 8 minutes or until a very light brown. Remove cookies to racks to cool. Makes about 6 dozen cookies.

DECORATIVE TOPPINGS

Ice with your favorite icing or brush cookies with heavy cream or with a mixture of one egg white slightly beaten with one tablespoon water. Sprinkle with sugar, nonpareils, chopped nuts, shredded coconut, cut-up gumdrops, or butterscotch pieces.

IFS, ANDS, AND NUTS COOKIES

2 cups flour

2 teaspoons baking soda

1 cup butter

1 ½ cups packed brown sugar

½ cup granulated sugar

1 ¼ cups chunky peanut butter

2 eggs

1 cup chopped, unsalted, twice-roasted peanuts

2 ½ cups semisweet chocolate chips

1 cup peanut butter chips

Preheat oven to 350 degrees F. Do not grease cookie sheet.

Sift together the flour and soda. Set aside. Beat butter, sugars, and peanut butter in a separate bowl until fluffy. Add eggs and dry ingredients and mix well. Stir in peanuts, chocolate chips, and peanut butter chips. Shape into small balls and place on an ungreased cookie sheet. Flatten with a glass dipped in sugar or make a crisscross with a fork. Bake 8 to 10 minutes. Makes 2 ½ dozen cookies.

Lion House sugar jar.

STING OF THE BEE (BIENENSTICH) CAKE

Prepare topping and allow to cool while preparing cake.

TOPPING

- ½ cup butter (no substitutes)
- ½ cup sugar
- 2 tablespoons milk
- 1 cup slivered, blanched almonds
- 2 teaspoons vanilla extract

In medium saucepan, melt butter until almost boiling. Add sugar and bring to a boil, stirring constantly. Slowly add milk; stir carefully, as mixture will pop. Return to a boil and add almonds. Bring to a boil once again. Remove from heat and stir in vanilla. Allow to cool to room temperature if made early in the day; or cool in refrigerator until thick and cool to the touch. For best product, topping should be same temperature as dough when used.

CAKE

1 cup butter (no substitutes)	1 tablespoon baking powder
⅔ cup sugar	1 teaspoon salt
2 eggs	½ cup milk
3 cups sifted flour	

With mixer, cream butter and sugar until soft; add eggs and mix well. Mix in flour, baking powder, and salt; slowly add milk. Beat until dough is thick and does not stick when touched.

Prepare 10-inch springform pan: Place parchment or waxed paper on bottom of pan. Attach side of pan; spray side with nonstick cooking spray and lightly dust with flour.

Press dough evenly in bottom of springform pan. Sprinkle small amount of flour on top of dough; gently tap dough down with flat bottom of a cup. (Dough should feel firm and press against the sides of pan.) Pour topping on dough and spread evenly. Cover pan with foil and bake at 375 degrees F. 30 minutes. Remove foil and bake an additional 10 to 15 minutes, until cake looks firm and golden brown. Allow to cool. Split in half horizontally, fill with Buttercream Filling (below) and raspberry preserves.

Note: This cake is similar to biscuits in texture.

BUTTERCREAM FILLING

1 cup butter (no substitutes)

2 cups powdered sugar

2 egg yolks

2 teaspoons vanilla extract

½ cup raspberry preserves

Soften butter. Beat in powdered sugar, egg yolks, and vanilla until fluffy. Spread on bottom half of split cake. Spread preserves on top of butter cream and replace cake top.

CHOCOLATE CREAM CAKE

CAKE

> 1 (18- to 18.5-ounce) package devil's food cake mix

Prepare and bake cake according to package directions for two 9-inch round layers. Cool and split cake layers horizontally. Only 3 of the 4 layers are used in this recipe. Freeze extra layer for later use.

STABILIZED WHIPPED CREAM

> 1 envelope (1 tablespoon) unflavored gelatin
>
> ¼ cup cold water
>
> 3 cups heavy cream
>
> ¾ cup powdered sugar
>
> 1½ teaspoons vanilla extract

In a small saucepan, combine gelatin with water; let stand until gelatin softens, about 5 minutes. Place over low heat and cook, stirring constantly until gelatin is just dissolved. Remove from heat and allow to cool slightly, but do not allow to thicken. In a large mixing bowl, whip cream, sugar, and vanilla until slightly thick. On low speed, gradually add gelatin, and then beat on high until cream is thick and peaks hold their shape.

CHOCOLATE FROSTING

> 4 tablespoons cocoa powder
>
> 3 cups powdered sugar
>
> ¼ cup butter or margarine, softened
>
> 2 to 3 tablespoons milk
>
> 1 teaspoon vanilla extract
>
> 2 tablespoons chopped walnuts, optional for garnish

COCONUT CREAM PIE

½ cup sweetened, flaked coconut

1 (9-inch) pastry shell, unbaked

3 eggs, slightly beaten

¼ cup sugar

¼ teaspoon cinnamon

¼ teaspoon nutmeg

¼ teaspoon vanilla extract

⅛ teaspoon salt

½ cup half-and-half

1¼ cups milk

Spread coconut evenly in bottom of unbaked pastry shell; set aside. In separate bowl, beat eggs slightly; add sugar, cinnamon, nutmeg, vanilla, and salt. Mix well. Mix in half-and-half. Add milk and mix thoroughly. Pour over coconut and bake at 400 degrees F. 50 to 55 minutes or until knife inserted near center comes out clean. May be served warm or chilled, topped with whipped cream, if desired.

Silver tea service.

VERY BERRY PIE

Pastry for two 2-crust pies
1 bag (16 ounces, no sugar added) frozen boysenberries
1 bag (8 ounces, no sugar added) frozen blueberries
1 bag (8 ounces, no sugar added) frozen raspberries
1¾ cups sugar
½ cup cornstarch
½ teaspoon salt

Line 2 pie pans with pastry and set aside.

Thaw all berries; pour berries with their juice in mixing bowl. In separate bowl, mix sugar, corn-starch, and salt; pour on top of berries. Mix well with rubber spatula. Fill pastry-lined pie pans, add top crusts, and bake at 375 degrees F. 45 to 50 minutes or until golden brown. Makes 2 pies.

Glass pitcher.

The Lion House parlor in 1943.

INDEX